Free Verse Editions
Edited by Jon Thompson

A SUIT OF PAPER FEATHERS

Nate Duke

Parlor Press
Anderson, South Carolina
www.parlorpress.com

Parlor Press LLC, Anderson, South Carolina, 29621

© 2023 by Parlor Press
All rights reserved.
Printed in the United States of America
S A N: 2 5 4 - 8 8 7 9

Library of Congress Cataloging-in-Publication Data on File

978-1-64317-361-0 (paperback)
978-1-64317-362-7 (pdf)
978-1-64317-363-4 (ePub)

1 2 3 4 5

Cover photograph by _____
Book design by David Blakesley.

Parlor Press, LLC is an independent publisher of scholarly and trade titles in print and multimedia formats. This book is available in paperback and ebook formats from Parlor Press on the World Wide Web at https://www.parlorpress.com or through online and brick-and-mortar bookstores. For submission information or to find out about Parlor Press publications, write to Parlor Press, 3015 Brackenberry Drive, Anderson, South Carolina, 29621, or email editor@parlorpress.com.

Contents

I. A Suit of Paper Feathers

    Fruits of My Labor *5*
    Projects Not Realized *6*
    On a Farm Near Junction City *7*
    After Tom T. Hall *8*
    Illinois River, Northern Arkansas *9*
    Damascene Scimitar *10*
    Radiant Archipelagos *11*
    And Her Red Hair Lights the Wall *12*
    Primm Meadow *13*
    Texarkana Apocrypha *14*
    Dragonfly Eats Her Weight in Time *15*
    One for Mister Whistle *17*

II. A Corncob Angle Measuring the West

    The Prime Mover *21*
    Garish Abstract Stained-Glass Birds *22*
    The Country's Best Yogurt *24*
    The Farm Boss Asks If I Plan to Wait Tables *25*
    Top Sod Ichabod and the Sermon on Data Colonialism *27*
    Hoary Glamour Rag *28*
    Sweathouse Falls, Bitterroots *29*
    Flat-Earth Antipodes with Ice Cream *30*
    Iceberg Lake *31*
    Positive Declination *32*
    Ministers of Automated Respiration *33*
    The Hermit of Foran Gap *34*
    Little Rock *35*

    Of Vagrant Dwellers in the Houseless Woods   *36*
    Dirtbike Cowboy Space Robbers   *37*
    Charles, Delete This Voicemail   *38*

III. I'm Ready for a Human Story

    This Is the Rate of Elation   *40*
    Per Your Email Re: Spider   *41*
    Resonance Disaster   *43*
    Peer Review   *44*
    Cadron Creek   *45*
    Two Rat Poem   *46*
    Amphetamine Poem 3   *47*
    Reliquary   *48*
    Bivouacked in the Valley of Your Dead Remark   *52*
    The Loneliness Inside Violence   *53*
    Wraith Croquet   *54*
    A Box of Light That Had Been a Tree   *55*
    Yard Turkey   *56*
    New Year's, Charles, Blue Ridge   *57*
    Dispatch from Pavements Grey   *58*
    Goodnight Poem   *59*

Acknowledgments   *61*
Notes   *63*
About the Author   *65*
Free Verse Editions   *67*

for Charles and Georgia

I doubt that Titian ever felt this rat gnaw.

—Virginia Woolf, *The Waves*

I. A Suit of Paper Feathers

Fruits of My Labor

When the emperor chained me to the gates
he said *you could've been my son*. I used
to laugh so—my friends would call me
a queen. I thought about this awhile, felt
regal and pale like a child's nail after you
remove its splinter—or the captain
of a light gunboat patrolling the coast,
calling you from the deck to say
Lucinda Williams sings like she isn't
trying to sing, doesn't she?

Projects Not Realized

Installation artists Christo and Jeanne-Claude
meant to cover miles of Arkansas headwaters
in silver canopies. Their axiomatic structure
would've dimmed sunlight in riparian biomes,
disrupted trout migrations, blocked the route
of wildlife to a high prairie's only water source,
eroded banks in parallel construction—the list
swells. In an alternate present, white rapids fade
as I float down the gorge on a blue plastic raft
and in the noon dark I miss my landing: a boulder
with a trailblaze and cairn on the beach. I'd meant
to camp there—with parachute cord and tarp
enough for shelter, I'd rest after the day's rowing
till the sunset melted on a lip of canyon. Instead,
I drift blind past that beach under one more
of the planet's smoke carpets. A parched cow elk
the artists didn't consult—practiced as she was
at scaling the canyon in a switchback of leaps—
lands on a canopy, rips its moorings, then falls
to the river in a silver-gray sack. I scull my raft
across the channel toward the sky museum
that's opened now above her grave, and pretend
I'm the docent—addressing tours of foam
with a drenched oar brandished at the sun.

On a Farm Near Junction City

Beside the rainy hog shed, the county food bank
forklifts pallets of old bread, blue with deep mold
and tints of February. In our slickers with knives
we slit packages of rancid buns, pre-made PB & J's,
their special rot an Oregon green—and feed it all
to the pigs. We feed them fetid eggs, decayed
chickens also, but today is bread day. Farm folk
say pig manure is the only kind with a bad smell;
it's the ammonia. We clean the pen with shovels,
push the slimy dreck to the slough. My colleague
and I, we scrape the floor till our filthy tools spark.
This guy's a real employee, speaks good Spanish
to the other hands; so, when he asks, *are you a man
of the herb?* I think I must be—a dim volunteer
shoveling his way to dinner. All this because
I should've followed some lover to Chattanooga
or learned to operate the track hoes in Arkansas
but instead I'm near the ocean, and broiled thoughts
cool in labor's mute thrum. After a shower, I'll listen
on the couch to the farm's daughter play Chopin
while a cat I've never met scales my chest, nestles
into sleep. A kind of recompense I think, for lives
we didn't choose—because winter's animal bed
needed fresh straw, or the woodstove in our bunkhouse
grew cold, and somebody had to get up and stoke it.

After Tom T. Hall

I'm nothing like a rabbit dog
in Carter County. You might tell
as much from my teeth or my
frail calves. I'm hard to motivate like
a zebra. Don't look at me I only want
my mom to like me. Together,
we take an insect walk to the low river.

Illinois River, Northern Arkansas

There's an old hayfield on the south bank
where a company of environmental mitigators
planted a new forest, built wetlands to replace
ecosystems destroyed for impeding operations
of frackers in the shale boom. As a laborer,
I helped men excavate new creek beds,
gird riparian zones in sandstone, wait for rains
to fill them—new homes where native species
of fish could spawn—and sowed the field
with grass and sapling seed. The land fragile
in July's drought, we worked every night—
set a pump in the river, hooked many links
of canvas firehose to sprinklers we'd rotate
through the rows in slow orbits till dawn,
rode home together in white trucks filthy
with the river's red clay. When the forest
grew stable, the company moved to distant
contract-acreage, but I held onto my key
to the property's gate. I'd bring friends out
for parties, and we'd spew gin at pyres
of rivercane to make it pop, turn useless
phonebooks into blazing trebuchet payloads,
sleep drunk on the ground in crackling beds
of cicada husks. In the morning, we'd rinse
each other's grass stains with iodine water
from the river. One night we saw big clouds
full of heat lightning advance, so we circled
in the field among the saplings, tallest objects
for a hundred yards—trying to become conduits,
termini of a black sky's ropes of fire, our faces
maps to wonder, rain-warped, useless now.

Damascene Scimitar

for W. H. Auden

In the man-shaped valley of your mattress:
a single line of round stones.

Chainsaw murderers tumble down bleachers.
It would complicate our work—

a curio, not a relic. *Not relics
but curios.* We slice through membranes

into clarity—*does the language
embody what it indicates?*

/

Here, an eagle named Barabbas
prepares to fake the rapture.

Hailstorms crunch through diamond mines.
The story about money

became a cosmology.
Nice to mourn you—

quips the round stone
in the man-shaped valley.

Radiant Archipelagos

Meet me at the sushi joint,
Hamilton, Montana—
I'll set it on fire so you can find it.
I'll fill the place with wolves
if you'd prefer. Either way,
catechisms on permanence
converge. Excellent news,
excellent news—I announce
as you lope toward me
and the glass door
reopened, skreeks—
2nd Street Sushi.

And Her Red Hair Lights the Wall

for Richard Hugo

Backpacking solo up the Bitterroots
    a woman spends the night
        in an off-season fire lookout.
She boils snow for mashed potatoes,
    eats them on a plywood cot.
        Later, she dreams of someone
    draping cobwebs on her face one by one
        like a pallet of veils. She wakes to realize
            she's been covered in white locks
    by a naked crone perched on rafters—plucking hairs
        and dropping them to float through shafts
            of dusty moonlight to the woman
    who flees in wool socks and sleeping clothes
miles down the mountain to some homestead, safety.

As Lisbet tells me this story
    her hair is a red inverted frame
        for the panoramic white of hills
around Missoula. The myth expands with a breakout
    at the shuttered hospital for the so-called insane,
a eugenics program to sterilize those deemed *manifestly unfit*—

    Lisbet stops to peel lunch apples with a knife.
Mountain wind cuts all my jackets, and I think
    if her story was true, inmates must've roved
        east in frail gowns from a now black-sited asylum
in Warm Springs, over the Flint Range
    and the Sapphires—how they must've passed
through Philipsburg to make the Bitterroot.
    Maybe the naked woman who sheltered
        in that lookout was once a town's *best liked girl*,
            slender, with hair bright enough to redeem
      some diner's manly tragedies by proxy—
        and each hair she cast on her sleeping guest
            fell as a hex on tourists in bad histories,
        compounded silence, the various babes
            a mountain sends—who I map in colors wrong.

Primm Meadow

In Gold Creek Basin
a ponderosa trunk's
ochre plates of bark
converge with black
fault lines we decide
smell like cinnamon.
I shoulder a blanket,
you the flask where
gin swishes. Rusting
historically, chassis
from settler wagons
are ragged beds for
Montana wheatgrass.
Sickle shadow moons
pock the ground via
an off-center eclipse.
The valley otherwise
charred, this glade is
old-growth miracle.
Behind an iron fence
of pointy fleur-de-lis,
sun-dappled pioneer
headstones could be
my ancestor's
ultimate colony.
Leaving, we passed
an SUV's worth of
dudes spraying trees
with semi-automatics.
It's national forest land
now. A citizen can do
whatever he likes here.

Texarkana Apocrypha

There used to be these famous turkey hunters—
twin sandy-haired brothers, thick linebacker hands
on twenty-gauge Benelli guns they saved for and bought
with yard money, kept clean and greased all year
so the barrels' painted wheatgrass camouflage
never dimmed—who'd go out together each April
to the big French Creek tract and split up. One
would stalk down on the flock from the north,
while the other, having driven around to the south,
made a silent lower jaw for a mouthful of feathers
closing. At the set time, they'd blow on box calls
to drum up hens in spring heat; and more than once
the brother's touch of kinship was shrapnel met
in the expert's zone of a bird heart from both sides.
One year, they mistook each other's calls for toms,
so when the twins shot blind at their prize's rustle
in high grass, they died with groans of hunted things—
and I know every Game and Fish office from Nebraska
to Florida has some local rendition of this story,
but I still remember being a kid, Elsie warning me
about those boys crouched in grass, not meaning
to hunt one another, cold shotguns pressed to faces
tensed for the kick, wondering if I was brave enough
to leap between them in my suit of paper feathers.

Dragonfly Eats Her Weight in Time

They cut ice with chainsaws   split their own footing

to make way for the barge   sunk chain to dock anchors

beneath a frozen lake   sent welders in black neoprene
beneath a frozen lake
beneath a frozen lake   hitched float pads to the rebar.

/

A kid with a nosebleed clung to the dock:
summer's wet jackal—open mouth frothed
with spit and foam and blood *stop*
laughing for one second, please.

/

On this island, acid seeps from pine roots,
turns soil to gray dust. The camp's director
won't pay for waste removal via barge—
and this is why we burn greased Styrofoam behind the mess hall.

/

    If the Swan Range foothills burn
and cries of newborn osprey coalesce into clouds of midges
       and quartermasters proclaim in addition to the nine deer we have a fox
           with two kits must've crossed over the ice—I walk a shale cairn path

to the firebowl beach. When I stack glacial stones in my left hand
       and skip them with my right—am I the clay pigeon launcher?
          Cancel the artillery rehearsal or get some nice rocks.
              Distant boaters? they'll never leave July.

/

The eagle preserve remains off-limits. Before the kids show up, I'll dive
a great many times, making different columns out of bubbles underwater:

(making different pillars out of bubbles)   (a scherzo of fire—except bubbles)
(a million paratroopers reverse the invasion)   (the souls of extinct birds may
   localize at random)

/

Instructions for guarding your first opaline mountain lake dawn:
paddle the wake of your best swimmer whose name is Adonai.
He is undrownable. He laps the island. He will remain ahead
of your canoebow. However, this is not to say it is acceptable

to stow the guard tube. Dam technicians
drain manmade lakes. Bleached effigies
of driftwood rot. Still, there is time to stop the maniac
before he splices DNA of rainbow trout—*paddle faster*

/

The kid on the dock stares at a bug fresh out of its cocoon. He tells me, "I put
my shoes around her so nobody would step on her, and now I have to wait
till she flies away." So I lay down on the dock to watch this bug grow with
the kid, and it starts at like, a few millimeters, and this kid is just sitting there
telling me all about bugs—"I think this is a stormfly, but it's pretty early for
them to come up"—and we're watching other stormflies crawl up the docks,
wriggle out of their cocoons and the first one—seriously you could watch its
wings grow like a time lapse and this kid is telling me all about *water creatures*
and the stormfly's wings kept growing and it became like a 2-inch long
dragonfly over the course of about half an hour then shuddered, flew off—et
cetera. You can see it on your own—
                       so make it eat some midges
                              have it contribute to the gene pool
                                      lead it toward a final predator—
                                            okay, good. Now do me.

One for Mister Whistle

When he whistled:

        a dynamo clicked in a distant room

        air seeped into shafts of feathers

        clouds broke apart, reconsidered

        sightless lizards tasted caves

        and began to scuttle faster—

        quite

        unprovoked.

When he whistled:

        barbarians stammered in molten tabernacles

        Venetian grottoes formed

        musk oxen heaved through snow

        wandering interlopers loped,

        glared at one another like they each had three eyes—

        each a moon of a moon

        of a moon.

II. A Corncob Angle Measuring the West

The Prime Mover

Between the pit of man's fears—
dog-chain algorithms, the party mushrooms stolen

and the summit of his knowledge—
cryodesiccation, flush toilets in space

my son trips over his ninja costume.

/

He may accomplish something so historical—
teenagers loitering in radiation shelters

contemplate the long-term repercussions
of smothering him as a baby. Meanwhile,

he's just here, twizzling flaps of elbow.

/

I am not terrified of sincerity
but what if he names his penis *Astrophel*?

"The heart is a litter of puppies
in the stomach of an alligator" he may reveal

at any time, from any pile of leaves.

Garish Abstract Stained-Glass Birds

The self-policing demographic of my back patio
        deserves a tax break. The word *phlebotomist*
is microwaved butter. The word *aperture* should be
        a vandal's snare, hid beneath monastic
flagstones. Free association puts you squarely
        in the aesthetic lineage of the President.
The word *thorax* ought to mean some elephant molar—
        ivory and brick-like, surely.

In metaphors involving skulls as geologic zones,
        the sinus cavity becomes the aquifer.
Morality begins as atmospheric pressure exerted
        on your zygote. In a ratio akin
to urgent car sex, bald statements counter *impossible*
        with *inevitable*. All suburb neighbor's
power tools sound like pissing robots. Isn't mortgage
        death gauge? I rent this ceramic birdhouse

but my adult daughters pay the water bill—
        extravagant showers, stepstool by the toilet
for their knees—incomprehensible geometries.
        No sound practice of aesthetic or design
informs our orientation—it ought to involve
        more water. If the future's limbless
archaeologist dusts nuclear ash from majestic slopes
        of my propane grill, it may declare

Ziggurat. Whatever those globular fan things are
        that spin near crests of subdivision roofs—
they are black pumpkins. My friend Collin says
        hallway thermometer when he means *thermostat*.
Electromagnetic saturation in the troposphere
        bloats everything except for animals—

if it's just one more allegory on diligence
        we're the bursting orchards, charmed—
and if the pronoun in *pronouncement* (one formal iteration
        past *announcement*) is just another iridescent glyph
duplicated perpetually in its linear ouroboros of light—
        a fountain's jet in a city with gravity—
we could both pretend it stands for *thou*
                              thou

The Country's Best Yogurt

In *his* house? a bedroom with spilled fishhooks
hid like animal traps in the shag rug.
A real pianola and its copper spool of braille—
sheet music for saloon ghosts. I'd stand
barefoot in the yard with a space rocket
themed popsicle. He'd shout my dead cousin's
name and I'd come running.

The Farm Boss Asks If I Plan to Wait Tables

When a flock blackballs a hen
they'll peck her to death inside
a week. That's why Melissa
swaddles this one on her lap
in a blue towel. She waves
to me from her cabin's porch
as I pass over a creek bridge
and up the mountain by some
rough directions: a ponderosa
       shaped like *this,* if you spot
              a fence like *that* you've gone
    astray. I thread tribal cattle
        in the back pasture. Beyond,
             a clear-cut slope recuperates
        into a furniture gallery. I take
            one stump on layaway, and
        my slicker is a drizzled pavilion
            I duck inside for cinematic
       Marlboros. Faint treeline elk
           accent the scene. Logging roads
      obey their own contorted laws
            inscrutably, and I stroll them
      toward an hour dark enough
   the farm sends a weary envoy
        on a rescue trip.

The driver says tomorrow's full
of dead ewe that need moving,
asks if I plan to help. I tell her
yes, imagining singular textures
of putrefied sheep, matted wool
squelching in a tractor bucket—
morbid sponges. The next day,
I'm sent instead to soviet blocks
of chicken coops, disgorging
vicious birds who peck open
each other's eggs to slurp yolks,
jab eyes of lifeless comrades
for protein—you really get

to loathe poultry. Feeding out
one ton of cornmeal to the flock,
I thought of this dude in some
lives-ago St. Louis who said
the best cigars smell just like barnyards
how that's a one-way contrast
and he'd likely never smelled
plywood vats and rancid meal
in a molted bog of feathers.
    After the feed, I visit a wolfhound
      named Liam Neeson. He's leashed
        to a stake between forest and coop
      and his world is a circular run.
        The rainswept sentry's eyes
      suggest all problems are contextual.
         Here, the camera pans to landscape—
     credits roll, and cellos complement
    my shrunken itch, a wet dog's ear.

Top Sod Ichabod and the Sermon on Data Colonialism

with a phrase from Yuval Noah Harari

"Your girlfriend's voice-activated essential oil
diffuser? an overpriced mole whose smoking ear
eavesdrops as it breathes, transmits frequencies
of mild desires, your fervent hopes (its bycatch:
sex and bathroom sounds) to leagues of silicone
meadow where exabytes of behavioral economists
roll about on refrigerated clouds. Soon, nothing
human will be unextractable for value. We'll graze
mobile panopticons as hackable animals, chattel
for technocrats suspended in vats of expropriated
serotonin," said Ichabod from his pulpit of defunct
pinball contraptions in the dive bar's miasma.

"But I'll be a darling balladeer of the new regime,
extolling intractable virtue of ten-century clocks
they've bored in desert mountains, their precise
and data-driven delineation of a snake throat's end.
Relay teams of Satyrs (biometric tethers blinking
on their hooves) shall blow me in a splendid palanquin—
amphibious, yet capable of subatomic getaways."
In this current of madness, I muttered to an eddy,
called a rideshare driven by an old man who said
It's amazing to watch people walking around
talking on their phones
it's like they're talking to Hariet the Rabbit or something

Hoary Glamour Rag

Lush valley marshes, tumescent clouds
swarm over calving glaciers in the moraine pool

(*Hoary glamour rag*)

    Isn't it good

when the bank transfer goes through

    "without a hitch"?

Take a break. *Touch* and agree.
    We'll be on this porch

"all winter"

    alone together like rich men.

/

I have seen the pseudoangels orchestrating language: " it was no one I expected "

    lush valley marshes, clouds

I dance in a beginner zone—

    pop the sequins from my gorgeous dress

      " like ice "

Sweathouse Falls, Bitterroots

The snake is an emended trauma,
the falls a starving anchorite
whose prayers I won't disturb.

Earth moves harder in the foothills.
The day is a pebble in its sling
        kinetic rock—
aimed at an upstairs window
in the house I'd just as soon
avoid a little longer—

where someone knows me like a faucet
(where I'm known like bathroom faucet knobs)
and the babies think they have my eyes.

Flat-Earth Antipodes with Ice Cream

with a nod to Donald Hall

My aluminum-free
        deodorant is made
of charcoal. Iterative
        self-perceptions slam
into one another with
        the incongruity of
perched hummingbirds.
        On the otherwise-
deciduous slope,
        cedars consolidate
the minority vote.
        My outdoor brain
is citronella mush.
        Pools of dew inside
a string light's bulb?
        they compare small things
        to other small things.

Location-agnostic, sunbeams fray.
        Things are bad now, but hives
of blackblue wasps are learning
        to eat these metal parasols
and build perfect houses, indestructible;
        their fluid nerve-stems resolute,
sped on flickering and silent wings—
        they'll keep enough of us alive
to raise pavilions just for rafters,
        joist elbows of pine where conic
        metropoles form.

/

In Montana, Polson girls ride horses to the ice cream shop.
Horse tails swish down Polson's empty main street—
three girls (on gigantic horses) saddles, bridles, tack
        all of it—
        they are *experts*.

Iceberg Lake

Snowmelt torrents through a mountain's gash
—louder for a silent alpine meadow, louder
for slowing waves of sound in frozen air.

Clouds grate like toppled boulders on the mist.
If you are fearful I am fearful; if serene, serene.
The deluge blasts the precipice with verbs.

Positive Declination

A comet and the bluegreen house
cord of lodgepole

side gate with its flaking slats—
hell is a bucket of soapwater

dousing anthills.

/

A comet like a mashed highlighter squeaks
over the porch. You could make water from ice,

graft dusk to a lilac bough.
If ever you return

you must tell us how it was with you.

Ministers of Automated Respiration

I am snorkeling out of a wet paper bag.

A Composition: "Ten Cups of Silver on a Stump in the Dale"

> *Well the crows they look like airplanes*
> *pleased to fall blazing out of the war*
> *when you're a blue rat*
> *preening its April feathers in the storm drain*

Some say I am like the souls of lunar impacts.

Some say I am as the bride is to the window.

The Hermit of Foran Gap

said he didn't much like to be called Ajax,
mentioned a certain inutile paratrooper
stuck on the cliffs up Fourche Mountain
and claimed he was my aborted brother—
but I think of my mom as a good catholic,
maybe a cedar tree's shadow in a cold snap.

Things he told me that I did believe: dogs
seize in dreams because they're fighting
our pain and losing; or when Cellar Spider
(daddy long-legs) loves Crane Fly, he'll lift
a veil from her proboscis while she strokes
his fangs; and those women the fates keep

a taut string of our lives to snip, *yes*, but also
envelopes with scabs off everybody's knees
left on girlhood's cul de sac in dusk. He said
shed antlers of elk used to peek through snow
back when this country knew seasons, and
the coffee stain on my map points toward kindling.

Making for camp, I fret the airman slung
off the cliff—little by way of solace 'sides
the jingle of carabiners in wind. I know
I won't find him in this lateness and dark
so in kindness I'll set no fire he'd see down at,
envy—*but what if he's a liar*

                                        Deserves It?

Little Rock

The Wednesdays in spring when they test the sirens

Every Wednesday at noon and the dogs answer back

Of Vagrant Dwellers in the Houseless Woods

Over heaped embers in the scarp nook,
shrimp thaw. Charles. Your iron skillet.
Pristine. Bad cigarillos. Nicotine-stained
fingers mix in David's blood. New cross
tattoo we're so curious. Stunted loblolly
speckle this cliff. Rope hammocks droop
above Lake Sylvia's dam and lost ravine.
Abandoned girl scout camp. Far cliff.
Doorless cabins moonlit, charm of 70's
masonry. None of us knows girls but
it's cool there used to be some over there.
Old enough for Mom's bible club now.
I whip together one pigtailed ghost from
promised raid, smoke air and summer dark.
Charles tightrope walks on dam crest over
big drop. There are six of us. Two flashlights.
Imposing cliff to scale. I have the ghost wail
distantly. We top out and flee nothing
over grids of blank foundation. What's it like boys,
bored again of deficient horror play?

Dirtbike Cowboy Space Robbers

Truck leaves wake on sunset
asphalt heat shimmer June
commute with Charles to
water trees tow light tower
for job site take Plumerville
exit onto 92 some dirt bikes
stuck behind us a pace when
helmet enters left periph shirt-
less dude green Kawasaki
oncoming lane this cowboy
flips visor glares two livid
brother eyes peels off now
I see the kid riding my blind
spot it was like the west a
good driver spooks bull just
before greenhorn is dashed
Charles skips a song I think
all brothers can whistle o
death or o vengeance it's
conjecture I crank the tower
winch Charles flips motor
switch the lights are black
holes building mosquito and
cricket galaxies cicada aster-
oids hit like paintballs sucks
shit don't it Charles let's go
rob banks you make up our
secret signal I'll get jetpacks
shades
lassoes.

Charles, Delete This Voicemail

Maybe I'll never see you weep drunk
into a campfire again because of your
impending baby—so I'll give you a ride
in a new Crown Vic, dog-walk you
to the Sunday races Arkansas. Maybe
I'll dress you as a pirate with seven
gold teeth and chain you to an anchor.
Maybe I'll whistle a dirge on the hilltop,
pen you a letter to ask *will you still
have time to climb every tree growing out
past the cliffs?* When you broke latex
in that sleeping bag, I guess you didn't
see the history museum is a one-man
county fair. I've hidden messages for you
under feathers of live canyon wrens,
coded onto their gray skin. It's probably
for the best if your child never finds them.
The name of my electric stove is Joan—
she warns me, "time is just a vampire
lacing her boots in the failed pavilion
of an empty state park." Charles I'd walk
to Memphis from the moon in a pair
of boat shoes if it meant I could turn you
back from a dad into the boys we swore
we'd stay—and hide you from the woman
you slept beside in woods without me
as a daughter crawled through calendars
grunting like a bear outside the tent.

III. I'm Ready for a Human Story

This Is the Rate of Elation

This is the rate of elation:
understand when I held fast against drywall
as if to boulder passage
between your work-life balance
and the empty seat
across the see-saw—

what if there's zero herons after death
what if *Zero Herons* was our band name
"zero herons understand strip mines"
I count zero herons when I raise my knees

(*zero* could mean several
(*herons* could be someones made of //

this is the race of elation:
shapes through shapes preceding.

Per Your Email Re: Spider

Watching pollen spume along one moth's
        heretofore
unmolested trajectory—
I follow the collapsing funnel
of element dust back
where mandibles knead.

This spider was never a Greek maid
        proud to challenge—

I've stolen the patents for calculus.
I'm eating paralyzed dirigibles
        at disparate coordinates
                in my filthy and concentric bed—
        also my house—
                also the 2D plane of the dead
superimposed, perpendicular
somewhere in the air beneath the eaves.

/

The large web taut between a flood bulb and a hummingbird feeder:
Light   sugar.

        Additional gnats fly to the web.   Most insects flounder
        up and down invisible switchbacks.   Not so much of light

        as delineating negative space—these fluttering piano chords—
        she spools them—embalms another thrashing moonlit bug,
        cauterizes nubs of web—preserving casual empiricism
        structural integrity—a mural of soundwave.

/

She's packing up now, she packs her playground and her toys
into a linear meat hammock. Her body is a synesthetic receptacle.
I'm ready for a human story:
>	*I wish you were different* I'll profess
>	to my bunkmates. My desiccated crickets.

Resonance Disaster

The city and its carousel full of raptors

Adult piñatas
Stuffed with coupons

Invisible craters you roll down

Sisters of men
With their cardboard tambourines

The carousel and its punctured horsies

—Look at us
Two pillagers

Our every word
"Septage Tanker"

"Earthling"
"Ankle Bone"

Peer Review

What vessel of history can be drained
in these instances whose proof
is only in their culmination
(subsequent filing)
?

The whole is not static.
Our dog-run of gravity is not static.
The page is a natural logarithm of aesthetic potential.
The point (1,0) is consistent in languages
intelligible to any two or more persons.

The aesthetic is a subordinate function to all history.
(History is fashion prevailing)
(History is fashionable ethics recalibrating)

Gargoyles nest
in the wing-clefts of stone doves—
a sketch from the workbooks
of your father's father,
that ~~judicious~~ mason
circumspect?
                        deathless

Cadron Creek

photos
of a great
blue tent
the Bronco's
downed tailgate
and its kerosene
hearth—even
when shown
the one of
Mom: short hair
and the smile
she'd lose with
the alimony—me
in her arms,
two soft child
fists full of the
river's best stones like
        invented toys—
inadmissible evidence
when I chose not to
believe her
        being too young
           to recall a family,
its elliptical rivers, weekends
that were supposed to work
/
parents must know they
exist to finish what they /
           begat

* I croon toward my litter of starving manticores
* a pink litter of manticores licks my paps raw
* manticores? man-faced, lion-bodied, scorpion-tailed
* (*scorpion*-faced, *man*-bodied, *lion*-tailed)

MY BRONCo's D O W N E D T A I L G A T E and its kerosene *hearth*
/ exclaims Dad??

Two Rat Poem

This is How I Would Hold You if You Began Transforming into a Moon Spirit:

the word *mauve* on the color mauve

small bubbles clustering a big bubble

mathematical hypotheses on neutron stars

tines of a leaf rake in a wad of leaves

deer ticks on Appalachian mice

poignancy on daffodils

epaulets on matadors

char on a mountain of Doug fir

paraphilic tendencies in roaches

rhythm on a plait of hair

propellers on the backs of manatees

special names for types of ships on ships (*caravel, barquentine*)

two rats in a cold sock—

Amphetamine Poem 3

I was eleven when he invited me to the lake house—
dirt road, gravel drive, slate walk.
My bicycle chained to the rail,
I grip a nylon backpack
in the sodium doorbell light.

Ms. Nelson opens the door like a porthole.
A wave of fresh bread escapes to the night.

I love the way my new dad feeds me,
how his ankle bracelet keeps him near the house.

/

Mallard wingtips break the glass lake dawn
and we prepare the fishing lines
impaling pink nightcrawlers
while our toes make words in the algae.

/

You tell me fish don't have eyelids, cast in shade.

I didn't want to start the electric knife
but you guided my hands just so.

And if I do this, can I watch the basketball playoffs?
After, of course, deboning the bream.

Their flaccid intestines in our paint bucket
glimmer like final alternatives.
It is taking longer than I thought. Thunderclouds blip.
I see now I can feed anyone.

Reliquary

for Charles Wright

1.

"Nothing moves at the speed of invisible cavalry"
you bravely proclaim
at the slightest provocation, even
when licked beneath azalea.

There's nothing coming for you.
You can't even straddle the mist in a torrent of sabers.

> **2.**
>
> If the ship you stormed in on
> and the dog sled you rode
> and the glass jar you appeared, finally, inside
> never amounted to much
> of an adequate chronology,
> the wake of seventeen—
> with its empty passenger seat
>
>   (ten thousand miles long)
>
> I pray your homily recalibrates.

3.

"Stars in Oklahoma are like pocks in a urinal cake"
chalks the master on the board
in the crenellated seminary.

Stars in New Mexico are a machinegun of tears.
Stars in Arkansas—the eyes of bats.
Stars in Montana—spilled bucket of nails
spilled on vats and vats of nails.

    4.

    In the desert—a Jenga tower
    of airstream trailers.
    Unoccupied: *For Lease*

5.

Some days feel like a champion stallion
trapped in the cave of a giant frog;
other shitty ideas
for coloring books.

"I didn't consent to being born"
says the tadpole
to the heron
during the moon—

    6.

    Heave, Heave, Heave Heaven
    up the shore, *up the shore*
    —drowned Heaven.

    My wife delivers trowels and pails.

    Get your sunblock we are grave holes
    and beachcombers—
    "extras in a seascaped infomercial"

7.

Feverish acolytes conspire
like baby monks.

Vaccines Work
suggests the pictogram

according to one interpreter.

Each night is a ritual trail.

8.

Each tree is a forthcoming crucifix.

Headlights could've been chandeliers.
Light pollution fucks owls.

I read the signs.
I check the oil.

This is a brand-new battery.
Leave a pillow on your couch.

Notes to Reliquary

    1—Dwarven Calipers
    2—Oseberg Wagon
    3—Harmonia's Necklace
    4—Flagstone of Buhen
    5—Hera's Thundercloud Shawl
    6—Scales of a Catoblepas
    7—Reed of Nekhbet
    8—Tail of the Cerberus

Bivouacked in the Valley of Your Dead Remark

I feel like the second draft of your astral projection.

Your veins are prophylactic Acherons.

It is time for horror to incite revolt.

Everything's preceding through our torsos

in the manner of javelin shafts.

/

" I have lied to victims and will kill again "

" chained black anchors on the tails of mermaids "

"and otherwise abetted the comptroller of dreams "

    —confess the young fathers

in a plea agreement with the state.

The Loneliness Inside Violence

In the dark, we sit close, appraising
negative space below stalactites
above stalagmites—
which, we assert, performs
the ghost of a stencil
the ghost of a cavernous stencil
black on black nothing
in a pitchdark cavern—
it spells interesting cave burbles
salamander minutes

                    (drip)

Listen, my darling—
if I stop breathing long enough,
I could ambush bats
and forlorn children in the upper passage.
We could really eke a living here:

((a feast of echoes

—the sound of hands in the dark
questing for the knife
eloping toward a wayward flashlight
burrowing in the air-colored mud
knuckling down cold warrens—

see? I call it a fist.

Wraith Croquet

> *You mention the danger*
> *and list the equipment*
>
> —Adrienne Rich

Three brothers at the wedding accost you:
    "This is what a virgin looks like"

Our bride is not cratered by taxonomy:
    "Implacable caterers drift across ballrooms"

Each guest is an *instanced* dialect:
    "We grew one eye for all our parents"

Our maids defend a bastion of cuisine:
    "And we are but vassals"

    Homing champagne ordinance
    Animal mothership

    A sortof wingspan

A Box of Light That Had Been a Tree

(They'll envy us for our delectable July)

(They'll begrudge us the ponderosa glade)

(They'll doubt our accord, how by its terms

I crossed the mountain with your tiger orchids)

/

I feel evangelical.
We should make a new language intelligible
only in its autonomous becoming,
intelligible only
to ourselves and pink embryos
wobbling in the swill of our collective translation.

/

We are not flayed skinless, miming awe
        atop some pike of *context*
on the ramparts of persisting Babels…

We should contort the whole tradition
        through the newest lens
and fill its lapsing narrative with dreams

Byzantiums of thought
        where at once the word *earthling*
flares in a shower of destiny
        spluttering its amniotic *why*

Yard Turkey

When I look at the turkeys in the yard
of our blue house—you molt on kitchen stools
awaiting forgiveness, as if justice lived
in the belly, and the heart was first
a raft of dredged cadavers lashed
to a bridge that couldn't build itself—

When I look at the turkeys in the yard
I don't get to meet David Berman
and my other clues amount to nowhere—
two echelons of prairie smoke
goose feathers stuffed in lungs
a sarcophagus with your name misspelt—

I realized today, looking outside
most of us are behaving.

New Year's, Charles, Blue Ridge

with a nod to C.D. Wright

When dawn's hunting party arrives
        steel crates unbolt in truck beds
                discharging hounds
who scent us in our frigid bags
        and we stir like reincarnated elk.

In the car defrosting, you mix cheese grits
        while I balance a camp stove on the console.
The trailhead's habitat to wild clans of ponies,
        non sequitur longhorn grazing shrub.
A logbook at the summit verifies our whereabouts.

We stomp ice in rain craters, glare spatially
        through Appalachian wind. Headed west,
we split up in Jonesboro like frontier marshals—
        embracing to hide our faces, one says *good luck*
                the other *happy trails*.

/

It didn't matter who wept first.
        Nobody gets to choose their allegory.
The night before those hunters showed,
        we formed a pagan circuit, careening
from beer stash to fire—sparks filled smoking vacuums
        in our blazing sashay's wake
and we fell in prone revel on frozen ground
        like two baron's dogs, curled by the hearth—
your dad is still my favorite church janitor.
        Will you let me hold your daughter?

Dispatch from Pavements Grey

I see a roller rink of moonlit water
for squat boys stacked on shoulders
in trench coats. Disguised as men
they skate the disco floor of lake—
fast across the vinyl, scree-stepping
clops of waves. In a hammock strung
from pines, needles spar above me
like bayonets with edges honed
on flaring whetstones. Ripples
fret sailboats till halyard clasps
chime against booms. The boys
speed to shore in hard stops—
disembark their stilted masquerade
and waddle back to stoic cots
pausing at the line near the boatshed
to hang their coats up next to mine.

Goodnight Poem

Even the suburbs were said to glint. We swapped
our dearest myths for piddles at bucolic open-air

swap meets. Brass steeple bells formed popular
crescendos in a model train city's alternative

microcosm. Democratically elected troubadours
harmonized—but we didn't keep these things.

They are rare now in the manner of operational
wheelbarrows. Small objects concretize absentia.

The moon has become an intimidating lozenge.
Disinfected newspapers provide further addenda

to our cryptic syllabus. I stroll diminishing perimeters
whistling elegiac nocturnes. Anything reasonable

feels like a trap. Hunks of satellite detritus align
to burglarize the silicate windows of a forthcoming

Mars mission. Stars embarrass my perspective.
Crickets abdicate their hegemonic chorus

to the passionate coyotes. I nap beneath a canvas
drop cloth of internal coziness. Luminous artillery

form batteries on distant ridges. Get under this
blanket—our hands could build a shadow town.

Acknowledgments

"Fruits of My Labor" appears in *The Offing* spring '21.

"Projects Not Realized" appears in *Granta* fall '20.

"On a Farm Near Junction City" appears in *Granta* spring '21.

"Primm Meadow" appears in *Paris Review* summer '22.

"Illinois River, Northern Arkansas" and "Texarkana Apocrypha" appear in *Southern Humanities Review* fall '20.

"Garish Abstract Stained-Glass Birds" appears in *Colorado Review* spring '21.

"The Farm Boss Asks if I Plan to Wait Tables" appears in *The Pinch* spring '21.

"Charles, Delete This Voicemail" appears in *Willow Springs* fall '21.

"Of Vagrant Dwellers in the Houseless Woods" won the 2016 University of Montana Poetry Prize as a previous version titled "Unlike Conquest."

"The Prime Mover" and "Flat-Earth Antipodes with Ice Cream" appear in *Green Mountains Review* spring '21.

Notes

Epigraph, p.iii: Virginia Woolf, *The Waves* (HBJ 1931).

"After Tom T. Hall": Inspired by Tom T. Hall's "The Fastest Rabbit Dog in Carter County Today".

"And Her Red Hair Lights the Wall": The poem plays on Richard Hugo's "Degrees of Gray in Phillipsburg" (1973).

"A Corncob Angle Measuring the West": Thomas Merton, *Raids on the Unspeakable* (New Directions 1964).

"The Prime Mover": The poem takes a couple lines from the original intro to *The Twilight Zone* (1959).

"Top Sod Ichabod and the Sermon on Data Colonialism": Yuval Noah Harrari, *Sapiens* (Harper 2015).

"Flat-Earth Antipodes with Ice Cream": Donald Hall, "Poetry and Ambition" (2005).

"Of Vagrant Dwellers in the Houseless Woods": William Wordsworth, "Lines Composed a Few Miles Above Tintern Abbey" (1798).

"Reliquary": Charles Wright, "Skins," *Country Music* (Wesleyan 1963).

"Wraith Croquet" epigraph: Adrienne Rich, "Trying to Talk with a Man," *Diving into the Wreck* (Norton 1973).

"A Box of Light That Had Been a Tree": The title is a line from an AI-generated "poem" devised by the Poetry Archive.

"New Years, Charles, Blue Ridge": C. D. Wright, *Steal Away* (Copper Canyon 2002).

"Dispatch from Pavements Grey": W. B. Yeats, "The Lake Isle of Innisfree" (1888).

About the Author

Nate Duke's work has appeared in *Paris Review, GRANTA, Colorado Review,* and elsewhere. He holds a PhD from Florida State University and an MFA from the University of Montana. A sculptor as well as a poet, he lives in Fayetteville Arkansas. *A Suit of Paper Feathers* is his debut collection.

Photograph of the author by Zach Hilty.
Used by permission.

Free Verse Editions

Edited by Jon Thompson

13 ways of happily by Emily Carr
& in Open, Marvel by Felicia Zamora
& there's you still thrill hour of the world to love by Aby Kaupang
Alias by Eric Pankey
At Your Feet (A Teus Pés) by Ana Cristina César, edited by Katrina Dodson, trans. by Brenda Hillman and Helen Hillman
Bari's Love Song by Kang Eun-Gyo, translated by Chung Eun-Gwi
Between the Twilight and the Sky by Jennie Neighbors
Blood Orbits by Ger Killeen
The Bodies by Christopher Sindt
The Book of Isaac by Aidan Semmens
The Calling by Bruce Bond
Canticle of the Night Path by Jennifer Atkinson
Child in the Road by Cindy Savett
Civil Twilight by Giles Goodland
Condominium of the Flesh by Valerio Magrelli, trans. by Clarissa Botsford
Contrapuntal by Christopher Kondrich
Country Album by James Capozzi
Cry Baby Mystic by Daniel Tiffany
The Curiosities by Brittany Perham
Current by Lisa Fishman
Day In, Day Out by Simon Smith
Dear Reader by Bruce Bond
Dismantling the Angel by Eric Pankey
Divination Machine by F. Daniel Rzicznek
Elsewhere, That Small by Monica Berlin
Empire by Tracy Zeman
Erros by Morgan Lucas Schuldt
Fifteen Seconds without Sorrow by Shim Bo-Seon, trans. by Chung Eun-Gwi and Brother Anthony of Taizé
The Forever Notes by Ethel Rackin
The Flying House by Dawn-Michelle Baude
General Release from the Beginning of the World by Donna Spruijt-Metz
Ghost Letters by Baba Badji
Go On by Ethel Rackin
Here City by Rick Snyder
Instances: Selected Poems by Jeongrye Choi, trans. by Brenda Hillman, Wayne de Fremery, & Jeongrye Choi

Last Morning by Simon Smith
The Magnetic Brackets by Jesús Losada, trans. by M. Smith & L. Ingelmo
Man Praying by Donald Platt
A Map of Faring by Peter Riley
The Miraculous Courageous by Josh Booton
Mirrorforms by Peter Kline
A Myth of Ariadne by Martha Ronk
No Shape Bends the River So Long by Monica Berlin & Beth Marzoni
North | Rock | Edge by Susan Tichy
Not into the Blossoms and Not into the Air by Elizabeth Jacobson
Overyellow, by Nicolas Pesquès, translated by Cole Swensen
Parallel Resting Places by Laura Wetherington
pH of Au by Vanessa Couto Johnson
Physis by Nicolas Pesquès, translated by Cole Swensen
Pilgrimage Suites by Derek Gromadzki
Pilgrimly by Siobhán Scarry
Poems from above the Hill & Selected Work by Ashur Etwebi, trans. by Brenda Hillman & Diallah Haidar
The Prison Poems by Miguel Hernández, trans. by Michael Smith
Puppet Wardrobe by Daniel Tiffany
Quarry by Carolyn Guinzio
remanence by Boyer Rickel
Republic of Song by Kelvin Corcoran
Rumor by Elizabeth Robinson
Settlers by F. Daniel Rzicznek
A Short History of Anger by Joy Manesiotis
Signs Following by Ger Killeen
Small Sillion by Joshua McKinney
Split the Crow by Sarah Sousa
Spine by Carolyn Guinzio
Spool by Matthew Cooperman
Strange Antlers by Richard Jarrette
A Suit of Paper Feathers by Nate Duke
Summoned by Guillevic, trans. by Monique Chefdor & Stella Harvey
Sunshine Wound by L. S. Klatt
System and Population by Christopher Sindt
These Beautiful Limits by Thomas Lisk
They Who Saw the Deep by Geraldine Monk
The Thinking Eye by Jennifer Atkinson
This History That Just Happened by Hannah Craig

An Unchanging Blue: Selected Poems 1962–1975 by Rolf Dieter Brinkmann, trans. by Mark Terrill
Under the Quick by Molly Bendall
Verge by Morgan Lucas Schuldt
The Visible Woman by Allison Funk
The Wash by Adam Clay
We'll See by Georges Godeau, trans. by Kathleen McGookey
What Stillness Illuminated by Yermiyahu Ahron Taub
Winter Journey [Viaggio d'inverno] by Attilio Bertolucci, trans. by Nicholas Benson
Wonder Rooms by Allison Funk

CPSIA information can be obtained
at www.ICGtesting.com
Printed in the USA
JSHW022139080123
35819JS00002B/93